Wolves

James Maclaine

Illustrated by John Francis and Kimberley Scott

Designed by Alice Reese

Wolf consultant: Professor David Macdonald CBE,
Wildlife Conservation Research Unit, Zoology Department, University of Oxford

Reading consultant: Alison Kelly, Principal Lecturer at the University of Roehampton

Contents

Top dogs

Wolves are wild dogs. They're the biggest and strongest wild dogs in the world.

These timber wolves are running through a snowy forest in North America.

Their long, powerful legs help them to run quickly.

Fantastic fur

Wolves don't all look the same. Their fur can be pale or dark. It can be long or short, too.

In winter, some wolves grow longer fur. This keeps them warm when it's cold.

They lose the long fur in spring by rubbing their bodies on the ground.

As a wolf gets older, its fur turns paler.

This Indian wolf
lives in the desert
where it's hot.

It has short fur that
keeps it cool.

Pack life

Wolves live in groups called packs. The wolves in a pack are usually from the same family.

There can be between two and twenty wolves in a pack.

This is a small pack of timber wolves.

The wolves in each
pack are different
ages and sizes.

A big male wolf
and a big female
wolf lead the pack.

They are called the pack leaders. They are
often the parents of all the other wolves.

Wolf homes

Wolves live in mountains, forests and deserts in different parts of the world.

This Arctic wolf lives in one of the coldest parts of the world where it's often snowy.

Its white fur makes it hard for other animals to spot.

A wolf pack lives in its own area of land.

The wolves move around the area together looking for food.

They choose a high, open place where they like to meet. They rest there, too.

If another wolf enters the pack's land, the pack chases it away.

Making smells

Wolves make smells to tell things to other wolves.

Wolves show where they live by marking the area with piles of smelly dung.

They spray on rocks and trees, and then spread the smell with their paws.

This wolf is smelling a rock that another wolf has marked.

Wolves share their smells with
other members of
the pack.

These wolves are from the same
pack. They're sniffing each other.

Team hunters

Wolves hunt animals for food. When a pack hunts together, it can catch big animals.

A pack sniffs the air and the ground. It smells a group of deer nearby.

The wolves chase the deer and try to surround the slowest one.

Suddenly, the wolves jump on the deer and drag it to the ground.

Wolves try to stay hidden from animals they're hunting by creeping up on them.

This wolf is teaching young wolves how to hunt.

It's showing them how to walk quietly.

Wolves use their good hearing to help them hunt.

Eating meat

The wolves in a pack take turns eating. They mainly eat meat.

The pack leaders eat first. They choose the softest and juiciest meat.

The other wolves fight over what's left. The weakest wolves eat last.

When there's no meat left, the wolves lick and chew the bones.

Wolves also eat berries, birds, fish and other small animals.

This wolf has caught a fish while hunting in a river.

Powerful paws

Wolves have big, strong paws. They use them for hunting and digging.

This wolf is hunting for mice hiding under the snow. It's trying to pounce on them.

Wolves save meat by burying it. They dig it up when they're hungry.

Before a mother wolf has her babies, she digs a den.

First, she digs a long tunnel into the ground.

Then, she makes a wide hole at the end of the tunnel.

When the den is big enough, the mother crawls inside.

Baby wolves

A mother wolf has around six babies at a time. Baby wolves are called pups or cubs.

The babies are born in a den. After they are born, the mother licks them clean.

They can't see or hear for a week. Then, they open their eyes and ears.

For the first two months, the baby wolves drink their mother's milk.

If a mother wolf needs to move one of her babies, she picks it up with her mouth.

She holds it very gently, so it doesn't get hurt.

 Baby wolves have blue eyes that turn brown, green or orange as they get older.

Growing up

As young wolves grow up, they spend more time outside the den. They start to eat meat, too.

Adult wolves swallow meat and take it to the young wolves in the pack.

The young wolves ask for food by licking and sniffing the adults' mouths.

Then the adults bring up the meat from their tummies for the young to eat.

Wolves learn how to hunt by catching small animals such as mice.

Young wolves play with each other. This helps them become stronger.

These wolves are learning how to use their paws while playing.

Lone wolf

Many wolves stay in their pack all their lives. Others leave their pack and live on their own. They are called lone wolves.

A lone wolf moves from place to place. Each day it has to find water to drink.

It also hunts for food. It eats small animals it can catch on its own.

If a lone male wolf and a lone female wolf meet, they might start a new pack.

Lone wolves try to keep away from wolf packs.

If a lone wolf meets a pack, they might fight.

These wolves are using their sharp teeth and claws while fighting.

Making faces

Wolves show how they feel with their faces and bodies.

These wolves are wagging their tails and licking each other's faces.

Wolves do this when they are happy to see each other.

 A pack leader stares at the wolves in its pack to show who is boss.

When a wolf is happy, its ears point up and its tongue hangs out.

If a wolf is scared, it bows its head down low. It also holds its tail between its legs.

An angry wolf snarls and shows its teeth.

It does this to frighten other wolves.

Noisy wolves

Wolves tell each other things by making different noises.

This wolf is lifting up its head to howl.

A howl is a long, loud wailing sound.

A wolf howls so other members of its pack know where it is.

When a wolf is in danger, it barks to call its pack to help it.

Baby wolves make squeaking noises when they want to call their mother.

The wolves in a pack often howl together to scare other packs. They also howl after they have been hunting.

Owhooo!

Sometimes, a lone male wolf makes loud noises to find a female.

Sleep tight

Wolves spend a large part of each day sleeping and resting.

When it's hot, a wolf sleeps on its side. This helps it to keep cool.

If it's cold, a wolf curls up in a ball and tucks its nose under its tail.

Sometimes, wolves stretch their legs and backs after they wake up.

These young Arctic wolves are sleeping side by side to keep themselves warm.

When they are resting, wolves sometimes clean themselves using their teeth and tongues.

Glossary

Here are some of the words in this book you might not know. This page tells you what they mean.

 pack - a group of wolves. Wolves live together in packs.

 pack leader - a wolf that is in charge of the other wolves in its pack.

 hunt - to search for, catch and kill animals, usually to eat.

 cub or pup - a baby wolf. A mother has around six babies at a time.

 den - the place where wolves are born and live when they are very small.

 lone wolf - a wolf that has left its pack, to live on its own.

 howl - a long, loud crying sound that wolves make.

Websites to visit

You can visit some interesting websites to find out more about wolves.

To visit these websites, go to the Usborne Quicklinks Website at **www.usborne.com/quicklinks** Read the internet safety guidelines, and then type the keywords "**beginners wolves**".

The websites are regularly reviewed and the links in Usborne Quicklinks are updated. However, Usborne Publishing is not responsible, and does not accept liability, for the content or availability of any website other than its own. We recommend that children are supervised while on the internet.

Wolves can swim. They swim across rivers while looking for food.

Index

Acknowledgements

Photographic manipulation by John Russell
Additional design by Sam Chandler and Zoe Wray

Photo credits

The publishers are grateful to the following for permission to reproduce material: cover © Daniel J. Cox/CORBIS; p1© Tom Brakefield/Corbis Flirt/Alamy; p2-3 © Jack Milchanowski/ Papilio/Alamy; p5 © John T.L/Alamy; p6 © Thomas Kitchin & Victoria Hurst/Design Pics Inc./ Alamy; p8 © Konrad Wothe/Getty Images; p10 © Jim Brandenburg/Minden Pictures/CORBIS; p11 © Corbis/SuperStock; p13 © Radius Images/CORBIS; p15 © Fabrice Simon/Biosphoto/FLPA; p16 © Jim and Jamie Dutcher/Getty Images; p19 © age fotostock/SuperStock; p21 © Christian Heinrich/imagebroker/Alamy; p23 © imagebroker.net/SuperStock; p24 © Picture Hooked/Malcolm Schuyl/Alamy; p25 © Terry W. Eggers/CORBIS; p26 © John Knight/Getty Images; p29 © Jim Brandenburg/Minden Pictures/FLPA; p31 © Frank Lukasseck/Getty Images